CELEBRATING CULTURES

THANKSGIVING

Faith Woodland

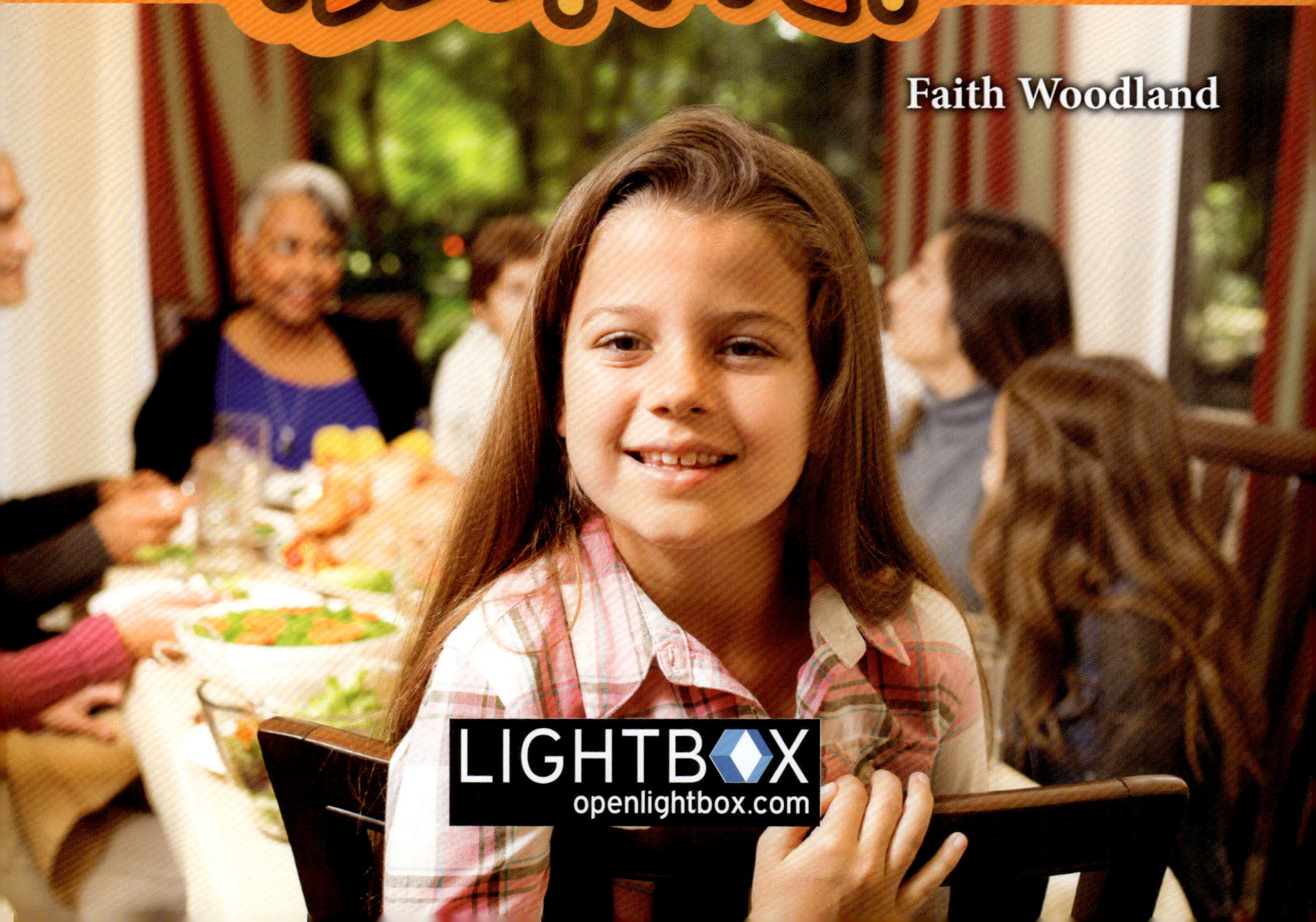

LIGHTBOX
openlightbox.com

LIGHTBOX

Go to
www.openlightbox.com
and enter this book's
unique code.

ACCESS CODE

LBXP6598

Lightbox is an all-inclusive digital solution for the teaching and learning of curriculum topics in an original, groundbreaking way. Lightbox is based on National Curriculum Standards.

STANDARD FEATURES OF LIGHTBOX

AUDIO High-quality narration using text-to-speech system

ACTIVITIES Printable PDFs that can be emailed and graded

SLIDESHOWS Pictorial overviews of key concepts

VIDEOS Embedded high-definition video clips

WEBLINKS Curated links to external, child-safe resources

TRANSPARENCIES Step-by-step layering of maps, diagrams, charts, and timelines

INTERACTIVE MAPS Interactive maps and aerial satellite imagery

QUIZZES Ten multiple choice questions that are automatically graded and emailed for teacher assessment

KEY WORDS Matching key concepts to their definitions

Contents

A Day to Give Thanks

Thanksgiving is a holiday in the United States. It began long ago when **Pilgrims** from England settled in the **New World**. As **Christians**, they thanked God for their first **harvest**. The Pilgrims also invited the Wampanoag Native Americans to share their feast.

Today, Thanksgiving takes place on the fourth Thursday of November. It is celebrated with a turkey dinner and fun activities. Friends and family often gather on Thanksgiving. They use this time to show their thanks for the good things in their lives.

Family and good health are just two examples of what people are thankful for on Thanksgiving.

More than **46 million turkeys** are eaten on Thanksgiving every year.

The average weight of a turkey purchased for Thanksgiving is **15 pounds** (6.8 kilograms).

A Feast in the New World

The first Thanksgiving in what would become the United States took place 400 years ago. Pilgrims from England came to the New World in 1620, on a ship called the *Mayflower*. They landed in Plymouth, Massachusetts. It was hard for the Pilgrims to settle the new land. The cold winters and food shortage made it difficult. They were helped by the Wampanoag Native Americans. The Wampanoag brought them corn and beans.

The Pilgrims invited the Wampanoag to a feast in the fall of 1621. One Pilgrim named Edward Winslow wrote a letter. He said that they ate wild birds hunted by the men. They ate **venison** brought by the Wampanoag. Berries and vegetables were also part of the meal.

The Wampanoag introduced corn to the Pilgrims. They did not eat it on the cob, but dried the kernels and ground it into cornmeal.

The Pilgrims and the Wampanoag feasted for three days.

Uniting the Country

Over time, people have told the story of the first Thanksgiving. The story started a tradition. In 1789, George Washington declared that the national Thanksgiving holiday would happen on the fourth Thursday in November.

Starting in 1798, the U.S. Congress let each state decide whether or not it would celebrate Thanksgiving. It was not until 1863 that President Abraham Lincoln declared Thanksgiving a national holiday again. Thanksgiving was used as a way to unite the country during the Civil War.

Sarah Josepha Hale spent 17 years writing letters to presidents, asking them to make Thanksgiving a national holiday.

As people go to grocery stores today, people in the 1800s would go to markets to find the food for their Thanksgiving meal.

Turkey Day

Turkey became the main Thanksgiving dish for several reasons. One is that turkeys are plentiful in the United States. Another is that one turkey is usually large enough to feed an entire family. It is also cheaper to buy than other meats.

Thanksgiving Timeline

The United States has grown as a nation over the last 400 years. Year after year, people remember how it began and give thanks. Thanksgiving has always been celebrated in November.

1621

The *Mayflower* Pilgrims give thanks to God for safety and food in the New World. They celebrate the autumn harvest with the Wampanoag people.

1789

George Washington declares Thanksgiving a national holiday.

1863

President Abraham Lincoln chooses Thursday, November 26, to be the official day to celebrate Thanksgiving.

1924

Macy's, a department store in New York City, has its first Thanksgiving parade. Three years later, the large balloons the parade is now known for are added.

1943

Artist Norman Rockwell paints a picture of an American family about to eat a turkey dinner. It is named *Freedom from Want*. People also call it *The Thanksgiving Picture*.

2019

More than 55 million people travel 50 miles (80.5 km) or more for the Thanksgiving holiday. This is the second-highest number of Thanksgiving travelers, after 2005.

Thanksgiving Today

Almost all Americans celebrate Thanksgiving. Most people gather with friends or family. Turkey is the traditional main dish. Stuffing, mashed potatoes, sweet potatoes, corn, **cranberry** sauce, and salads are common side dishes. Pumpkin pie is a favorite Thanksgiving dessert.

More than 3 million people attend the Macy's Thanksgiving Day Parade in New York every year. It is the largest Thanksgiving parade in the country. There are decorated floats and huge balloons. More than 50 million people watch the parade on television on Thanksgiving morning.

Cranberry sauce comes in two forms. It can be handmade from cooked cranberries or it can be jelly from a jar.

The **longest** balloon in the Macy's Thanksgiving Day Parade is **77 feet** (23.5 meters) long.

The **largest** pumpkin pie ever baked was **20 feet** (6 m) in diameter.

It can take up to 90 people to hold down some of the balloons in the Macy's Thanksgiving Day Parade.

Americans Celebrate

Many towns and cities across the United States have special traditions and fun activities for people celebrating Thanksgiving. These include parades and races. In some places, Thanksgiving also marks the start of the Christmas season.

The largest "Turkey Trot" in the country takes place in Dallas, Texas. More than 40,000 runners and walkers participate in an 3.1-mile (5-kilometer) race. Runners often dress up as turkeys.

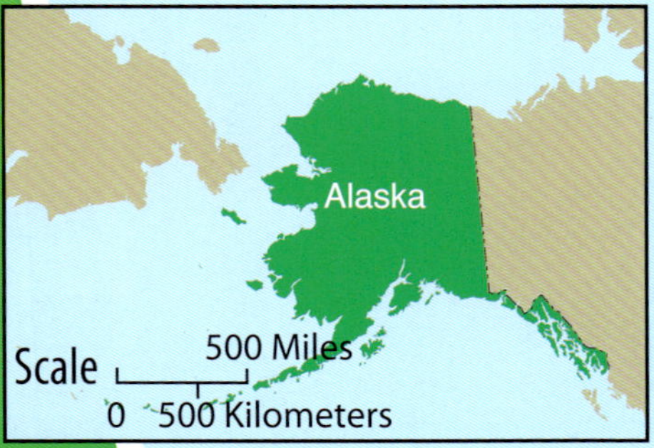

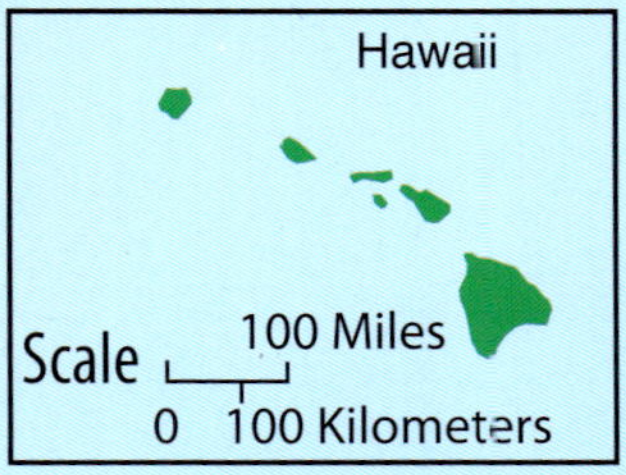

Philadelphia, Pennsylvania, hosts the longest-running Thanksgiving Day parade in the country. The parade first took place in 1920. Santa Claus has always been part of this celebration. There are also floats and musical performances.

Thousands of people in Plymouth, Massachusetts, take part in parades and events in which they reenact parts of U.S. history. They dress as Pilgrims, Native Americans, soldiers, **patriots**, and **pioneers**.

Chicago, Illinois, has a three-hour parade on Thanksgiving morning. There are floats, dancers, marching bands, and more. The city's Christmas tree is lit the Friday after Thanksgiving.

Each Thanksgiving, two turkeys are brought to the White House in Washington, D.C., for the official Turkey **Pardon**. The president pardons these turkeys, sending them to live out their days on a farm.

Food and Fun

A Bountiful Harvest

The cornucopia is a Thanksgiving symbol. It is a horn-shaped basket that is often filled with fruits, vegetables, and other foods. A cornucopia represents a plentiful harvest and an **abundance** of food. People often use cornucopias as a table centerpiece during their Thanksgiving meal.

The cornucopia was first written about in ancient Greek and Roman stories.

Cornucopias can also be decorated with flowers and tree leaves.

Playing games inside lets people relax and digest their large meal.

Playing Games

Many families relax after their Thanksgiving meal by playing board games or card games. If the weather is nice, families go for walks or bike rides. Football is also an important part of Thanksgiving for some families. A big college football game has been played on Thanksgiving since 1876. The National Football League (NFL) schedules several games on Thanksgiving as well.

More than 20 million people watch at least one of the three NFL games played on Thanksgiving.

Sharing and Shopping

Giving Back

Some families show their thankfulness by giving back to the community. Many people volunteer time on Thanksgiving to local soup kitchens or homeless shelters. They prepare and serve a Thanksgiving meal for those less fortunate or for people who might be alone on the holiday.

An individual homeless shelter can provide Thanksgiving meals for more than 1,500 people.

Shoppers spent nearly $70 billion over Thanksgiving weekend in 2019.

Black Friday

Thanksgiving is considered to be the start of the holiday shopping season. Black Friday, the busiest shopping day of the year, follows Thanksgiving. Stores have big sales on this day. Cyber Monday takes place the Monday after Thanksgiving. People receive special deals for shopping online.

Movie Magic

Many movies feature the Thanksgiving holiday. Some are more than 70 years old, while others are more recent. A few of the most popular ones are *Miracle on 34th Street*, *A Charlie Brown Thanksgiving*, *Garfield's Thanksgiving*, and *Home for the Holidays*.

Travels and Wishes

By Plane, Train, or Automobile

Traveling on Thanksgiving to see distant family has become a big part of the holiday weekend. College students look forward to going home to see family. Children visit grandparents and see cousins. People drive many miles (km) on Thanksgiving. Some take trains. Others fly in airplanes to visit relatives.

How to Travel

People have many different ways to get where they need to go for Thanksgiving. Millions of people traveled for the 2019 holiday. Some used cars, some used planes, and some used trains.

Planes

Approximately 4.45 million people traveled by plane.

Cars

About 49.3 million people drove and rode in cars.

Trains and More

Nearly 1.5 million people traveled by train, bus, or boat.

It is important to give the wishbone enough time to dry. If it is not dry enough, it will bend but not break.

Make a Wish

Breaking the wishbone is a tradition in many families. The wishbone is a bone in the turkey. It is similar to a human collarbone. After dinner, the wishbone is left to dry and become brittle. Two family members each hold a part of the bone and pull it apart. The person who gets the larger piece gets to make a wish.

Quiz

1 How did the Pilgrims come to the New World?

2 Where did the Pilgrims land?

3 Which Native Americans were at the first Thanksgiving?

4 In what year did Abraham Lincoln declare Thanksgiving a national holiday?

5 What is the painting *Freedom from Want* also called?

6 How many people traveled by car for Thanksgiving in 2019?

7 What is the largest Thanksgiving parade in the country?

8 Where does the largest Turkey Trot take place each year?

ANSWERS

1 They sailed on a ship called the *Mayflower*. **2** Plymouth, Massachusetts **3** The Wampanoag **4** 1863 **5** *The Thanksgiving Picture* **6** About 49.3 million **7** The Macy's Thanksgiving Day Parade **8** Dallas, Texas

Key Words

abundance: a very large quantity of something

Christians: people who believe that Jesus is the son of God

cranberry: a tart berry grown in the United States

harvest: gathering of crops

New World: a name given to the newly discovered American continent

pardon: the action of forgiving for an offense

patriots: people who support their country

Pilgrims: English colonists who traveled to a new continent in 1620

pioneers: people who explore or settle a new country or area

venison: meat from deer

Index

LIGHTBOX

SUPPLEMENTARY RESOURCES

Click on the plus icon ⊕ found in the bottom left corner of each spread to open additional teacher resources.

- Download and print the book's quizzes and activities
- Access curriculum correlations
- Explore additional web applications that enhance the Lightbox experience

LIGHTBOX DIGITAL TITLES
Packed full of integrated media

VIDEOS

INTERACTIVE MAPS

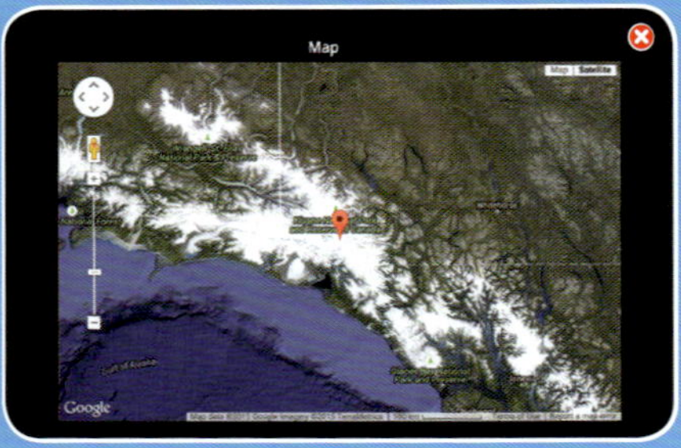

WEBLINKS

SLIDESHOWS

QUIZZES

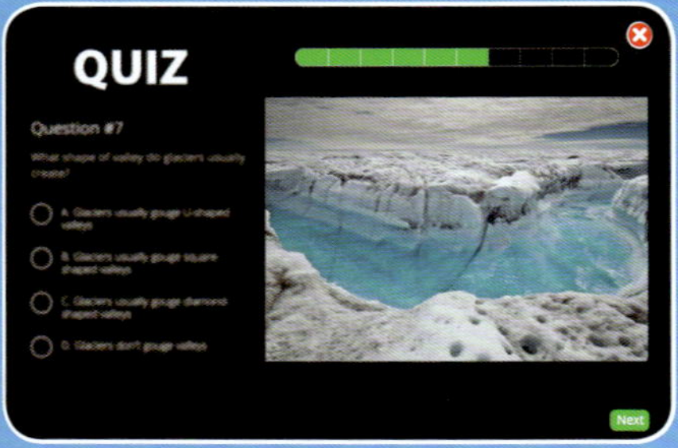

OPTIMIZED FOR

- ✔ TABLETS
- ✔ WHITEBOARDS
- ✔ COMPUTERS
- ✔ AND MUCH MORE!

Published by Smartbook Media Inc.
350 5th Avenue, 59th Floor New York, NY 10118
Website: www.openlightbox.com

Project Coordinator Heather Kissock
Designer Ana María Vidal

Library of Congress Cataloging-in-Publication Data
Names: Woodland, Faith, author.
Title: Thanksgiving / Faith Woodland.
Description: New York, NY : Smartbook Media Inc., 2021. | Series: Celebrating cultures | Includes index. | Audience: Ages 8-12 | Audience: Grades 2-3 |
Identifiers: LCCN 2019057151 (print) | LCCN 2019057152 (ebook) | ISBN 9781510553330 (library binding) | ISBN 9781510553347
Subjects: LCSH: Thanksgiving Day--Juvenile literature.
Classification: LCC GT4975 .W66 2021 (print) | LCC GT4975 (ebook) | DDC 394.2649--dc23
LC record available at https://lccn.loc.gov/2019057151
LC ebook record available at https://lccn.loc.gov/2019057152

Printed in Guangzhou, China
1 2 3 4 5 6 7 8 9 0 24 23 22 21 20

042020
111019

Photo Credits
Every reasonable effort has been made to trace ownership and to obtain permission to reprint copyright material. The publisher would be pleased to have any errors or omissions brought to its attention so that they may be corrected in subsequent printings. The publisher acknowledges Alamy, Getty Images, iStock, and Shutterstock as its primary image suppliers for this title.